The Heart Wants

poems by

Christina Quintana

Finishing Line Press
Georgetown, Kentucky

The Heart Wants

Copyright © 2016 by Christina Quintana
ISBN 978-1-944899-35-6 First Edition
All rights reserved under International and Pan-American Copyright Conventions. No part of this book may be reproduced in any manner whatsoever without written permission from the publisher, except in the case of brief quotations embodied in critical articles and reviews.

ACKNOWLEDGMENTS

Grateful acknowledgement is made to the editors of publications in which these poems first appeared:

First Class Literary Magazine:
"Painting" & "Bushwick Avenue-Aberdeen Street"

Foglifter:
"After Garner," "Al," & "Live Like the Geraces"

jdbrecords blog:
"Alchemy" & "King or Queen(tana)"

Saw Palm:
"Cornflakes con Leche"

Raspa Magazine:
"January," "Love's Equation," & "Reunion"

Grateful acknowledgement is made to the artistic director of Emotive Fruition, where the following poems were first performed, as well as published in the chapbook anthologies *Emotive Fruition + Radiolab: Elemental Poetry for the Masses* and the *Emo Fru All-Star Book of Poems*: "O," & "Letter to the Hearts I've Broken."

Editor: Christen Kincaid
Cover Art: Christina Quintana
Author Photo: Jorg Meyer
Cover Design: Elizabeth Maines

Printed in the USA on acid-free paper.
Order online: www.finishinglinepress.com
also available on amazon.com

Author inquiries and mail orders:
Finishing Line Press
P. O. Box 1626
Georgetown, Kentucky 40324
U. S. A.

Table of Contents

Love's Equation 1

Al 3

O, ...4

Neon 5

Cornflakes con Leche 6

From Her Going Away— 7

Letter to the Hearts I've Broken 9

Alchemy 11

Marathon 12

Live Like the Geraces 13

Painting 15

King or Queen(tana) 16

January 17

Sisters, Secrets, Legacy 18

After Garner 20

Pilgrimage 22

Bushwick Avenue-Aberdeen Street 23

More Time 24

For SMS
who knows it

Love's Equation,

*The Fredholm integral equation of the second kind,
may be solved as follows:*

I.   *Touch*

One smooth, clammy hand reaches shly for a cold fist-in-lap
below a painted wooden table
& soggy chicken sandwich
at Santa Fe Bread Co.

II.   *Sight*

Emerging from the subway in Crown Heights,
two balloons, high on sex,
into the white-hot sun,
on the day of the West Indian Day Parade

(I) and (II) expanded becomes an equation with:

III.   *Smell / Taste / Sound*

Desire, ripe like laundry,
fresh from the dryer

Weekends of sweetest sugar,
gallons of crisp craft beer

Laughter, singular, like
Adelie penguin calls to their mates—

So the solution becomes:

IV.   *Touch / Sight / Smell / Taste / Sound*

Swirling absent fingers
through lank hair

Eyes, dialed to moons;
explosions of silver

One garlic-soaked kitchen
mid-October

Resplendent raisins
in the picadillo

Side-by-side steps
in pavement conversation—

$$/ \ / \ / \ / \ /$$

We can compare the roots of this equation
in order to find the maximum
of their absolute values:

slick
bright
smokey
bitter
cacophonous

The solution is an infinite series.

Al

You share histories & futures,
Alabama, aluminum:
once, so silvery white.

Ductile as your drawl,
you rise: refined, recycled;
wanting change, nursing it.

O,

I needed you.

I grasped for you, your doppelganger—air.

You were lost, triangulated in my throat,
as I fell to the cold, hard tile.

Come back to me,
come back, please.

Neon

I saw the world in early 90s,
illuminated like magic of childhood & summer;
Ephemeral as thin tube wristbands filled with your essence for a one-night stand.

In adulthood, at my wintery desk,
I long for your electric, your fluid, your bright.

Cornflakes con Leche
Para mi abuela

1. Her apartment was bare and smelled like black beans. Black beans and the 1970s. I imagine if you could bottle up Washington Heights from that decade, it would have the same smell.

2. When we came by her place, she'd have Cornflakes waiting for me on the table—because she thought that's what American children would like to eat. I loaded them down with sugar every time, but the sugar sunk to the bottom of the bowl, clouding the powdered milk Abuela had, by magic, turned into liquid the night before.

3. She always smiled like she was sorry that a smile was all she had to give me, but it was all she had— she'd given everything else.

4. She loved Dad, my sister, and me, with all her heart, but I think she always felt like a stranger, too.

5. Her English was fine, but I think it scared her. She avoided the words, the looming burden of the life she carried here.

6. I can still see her in her signature outfit—some sweat suit Mom ordered for her from a catalogue years ago. She was never athletic, but that's all she ever wore for as long as I knew her. Her semi-gray black hair tinged with silver. And thin. She was so thin. Like she was barely there.

7. There we were in her empty kitchen—which she rid of all unnecessary objects so as to prepare for death—and she stood and watched as I crunched away at my cornflakes.

From Her Going Away–

[1]

I saw her photo and heard the party in the background—
                      I could still hear her voice so clearly
It stung; the sound, the memory of it.

Everyone was blurry, drunk, laughing:
There was nothing to mourn then,
This was a send-off, a farewell for adventure,
a mostly happy occasion of see-you-soons.

How to wrap your mind around a stumble-through,
a miscalculation, an oversight, an error—

It must be,
or the world's just humid with senselessness.

There are only more too many questions;
the windows are desperately fogged.

[2]

Showtunes for miles in that basement bar
where we gather for one reunion-in-loss;
the sort none wants, but everyone's grateful for—
because "I haven't seen you in _____."

And the lyrics dance right but wrong, in funny harmony,
because the heart matters more than the words.

And why mind that he can't play the title song
from *Sweet Charity*

it's only a song

And isn't the story in the singing,
the raucous, tipsy words spit from us all?

They hug us tonight like no one can
when arms have their limits.

Letter to the Hearts I've Broken

Dear Hearts,

Thank you for teaching me how to ride a bike in traffic. For being patient with my fear. For peeling me off the sidewalk when I flew over my handlebars, and helping me clean my wounds. Thank you for walking slowly beside me when I was failing at crutches– even when you were late for work and a block took a year.

Thank you for riding so many local trains from Sunset Park all the way to Inwood just to see me.

Thank you for kissing me back, for filling me with a clarity like none I'd ever felt before, for stealing sleep I never needed, for learning with me what it meant to love a woman.

Thank you for passing notes backstage on torn sheets of computer paper and sitting with me at a coffee shop late into the night talking books and plays.

Thank you for introducing me to your family, for telling them you loved me. Your homemade holiday cards were perfect.

Thanks for telling me I was the cutest girl at Pride.

Thank you for surprising me with expensive bottles of orange juice from Union Market when your bank account was running on empty and rent was an eternal obstacle.

Thanks for making me realize the beauty of sharing quiet with someone on the stretch of highway between Albuquerque and Santa Fe.

Thanks for sass with those hashbrowns. And the song—what a beautiful song. (I listen to it often.)

Thank you for not letting me drive away without a conversation, for sitting with me on the empty quad, for looking at me like I was the only thing that mattered.

Thanks for showing this carnivore how tofu can taste delicious when prepared with the right dose of soyrizo and salsa.

Thank you for wanting to know me, even after I broke your heart.

Thanks for telling me, *I hate to say it, but you're probably just the person who made her realize what she wants, and now she'll go on and get it.* I hope you know that you were so much more than that to me.

Yours,
CQ

Alchemy.

When I think of you,
I write bad poetry
teeming with enough feeling
to turn it to gold

When I think of you,
I recall why love is important
down to the early morning resin
of chapped lips and no sleep

When I think of you,
I forget that it's foolish;
I lose my sense of heartbreak;
I pummel through the stream of lights
as they shift to red,
kiss my hand,
and tap the roof of my proverbial car–

When I think of you,
I hear myself.

Marathon.

You're a tall glass of hope;
a row of stanzas
with a dash of boozey milkshake.

The course caked
with something sweet
and a welcome curl
at the top righthand
corner of its page.

5K, 10K, all the way
to the flagged line
at the back of my heart.

It's a quiet thing:
The sweat-drenched pulse
of finding you finding me.

I fell for the poem
before I knew you were it.

Live Like the Geraces.

> *"He gave a soft voice of life that comes when everything that happens is difficult."*
> —Narration from my dream

1. Today my neck is the ball of tightly wound rubber bands that sits in the 1/4 cup in my cupboard– or, the rush hour subway car, like the time that gentleman dove into the mass, sent me twirling like an unwrapped mummy inside of a Jello mold, and landed me inside a serious woman's armpit.

2. My heart is an elderly blind man blinking behind a teenage girl's pair of flashy shades. My shoulders are boulders at the edge of the sea—a beautiful, inescapable sea—that pounds energetically against their edges. A reminder, an urging.

3. My eyes are metallic. For the day they have replaced my nose and I can taste what they see. What they see is the want for something, the moment before, the hunger that taps away at the sidewalks, the street corners, of this place.

4. I think about what it means to be human and how, particularly, people often pronounce it as "u-man." Why is that? Where does it come from? Once it came from my sophomore religion teacher, who also said: "Anger is not necessarily a sin. Want for change can and should provoke anger to spark action, however, when the anger hardens into rage or hate, then it becomes sin."

5. I want life to taste like nachos—the kind you get from the Chinese-Mexican place around the corner and are so bad they're good.

6. I don't want to forget to travel. I want to make art and still afford to take my girlfriend out to dinner. I'd like a world where "day job" isn't a part of anyone's vocabulary and everyone goes to the theater. And it's free.

7. I wish for everyone to fall in love and be in love and to have someone to hug hard when the breaking part comes.

8. What would it mean for everyone to have a summer vacation? When the French aided us in the Revolution they should have insisted we take the month of August off, too. The vacation alliance.

9. I want for everyone to live their lives like the Geraces, who know what it means to live. What it means is believing and traveling and laughing and loving and treating everyday as an excuse for an adventure. Even if the adventure involves an in-town GPS scavenger hunt—and sometimes it does.

10. I'd like to feel more like the snowflakes that paraded across the sky today. They didn't know they were in New York and they didn't care. They danced effortlessly before my eyes—and I loved them for it.

Painting

It's raining lightly—
It's Park Slope, but feels like
an old movie you can't remember the name of, or
one of those street scenes in a frame at Stein Mart:
The kind you're embarrassed to love.

The waitress runs after us with my blue umbrella,
a peace offering, a thank you for being two women on the verge
of romance—
and a thirty dollar tip.

This must be what impressionism feels like.

King or Queen(tana)

My last name
is different from yours,
though it looks the same

I see you—the little boy—
dreaming of sailboats and horses,
but becoming a doctor, instead;
covered up in other
with no way out

Oh, if I could take your hand,
you there, floating in sadness,
and tell you in perfect Spanish
that you are enough

No, your Jesus-colored skin
couldn't save you,
but it didn't make you wrong

January

So many plans lead to solitude,
and then, the wind with its tongue-lashing,
the parental *I told you so*,
but colder, stronger.

Some things are inescapable,
even at a many-hundred
miles above the Mason-Dixon line.

Weddings being had,
babies being born,
and you in the front row
of an opera downtown.

Maybe their lives
were never yours to have.

Sisters, Secrets, Legacy

They were legitimate,
lacking syndromes spoken and unspoken,
so they came to America.

"This is your sister,
she will stay here
because her mother
was too old and
too mulatto
to make my wife."

They were educated,
by English-speaking nuns
with harsh words
for Spanish chatter
and uniform violations.

"I can afford only
to think of her
on a cook's salary
in Midtown."

They were married and umarried,
child-rearing and childless,
carrying accents that marked them like skin tone.

"I will go,
an old man in Brooklyn,
father to two, and not of one,
never knowing her fate."

They were citizens,
living and dying,
forgetting her name like Cuba herself.

After Garner

We all know
Manhattan is
the center of things

Which is why
The scene of the crime
is desolate tonight.

What if we all could,
sweetly, ever-so sweetly,
remove our winter gloves
and hold hands like
the two-toned sweethearts
sharing corner seats
on the subway?

Instead car horns cry,
keening for another one lost,
before another three and four.

Protestors' fingers frozen,
Police line corners;
pizza-in-hand, laughing like on holiday,

though a man is dead
and another is free,
and however many
little lights line
the stores and trees and skies,

it doesn't feel
one bit like Christmas.

Pilgrimage

I'm on the side of the road

All of the alcohol
in all of the bottles
and all of the everything

all of us were there:
every you that shared my bed,
and kissed my lips,
and believed that I was beautiful

"pork for the gentleman,"
and I blushed, and I loved it

would you believe she wore dresses
would you believe

Bushwick Avenue-Aberdeen Street

today thirty means mortality

but never mind sitting on the floor
and sharing beer from the bottle

these are the good old days
the ones that will shine on in
gold-tinged nostalgia,
like leaves

let's *pash* like the Aussies do;
how I prefer
to kiss with an accent—
and so what if it's mine?

More Time

It was supposed to be a snow day,
and it did snow, and they scraped
the streets and sidewalks
with a scratch/scratch/scratch
that reminded us we were alive
and awake and wanting;
enough to shimmy down the
hall, to fill our coffee cups
with knock-off Bailey's, and
side-by-side e-mail from home.

It was supposed to be longer,
her life; one that bloomed
the way wildflowers do
in the cracked sidewalks
of New Orleans, and had
many opening nights,
and five-borough love affairs
steeped in a wedding
on a sleepy-beautiful
piece of land in Connecticut.

We needed more time.

Christina Quintana is a writer and theatre artist with Cuban and Louisiana roots. Her poem "He-lium" was recently featured on Radiolab's "Elements" episode in collaboration with Emotive Fruition and her writing has appeared in *Nimrod International Journal, Gaslight: A Lambda Fellows Anthology, First Class Literary Magazine, Saw Palm,* and *Raspa Magazine.* Her plays have been developed and produced in Atlanta, New Orleans, and New York City, where she curates the Live Lunch Series, lunchtime theatre catered to workplaces. She is the recipient of fellowships from Lambda Literary Foundation and Columbia University School of the Arts, where she received her MFA in Playwriting. For more, visit cquintana.com

www.ingramcontent.com/pod-product-compliance
Lightning Source LLC
Chambersburg PA
CBHW060227050426
42446CB00013B/3204